Tyneside's Great War

Vanessa Histon

Tyne Bridge Publishing

Published by:
City of Newcastle Upon Tyne
Newcastle Libraries
Tyne Bridge Publishing, 2015
www.tynebridgepublishing.co.uk
Design: David Hepworth

All images are from Newcastle Libraries unless otherwise stated.
Front cover: Victory celebrations at Duke Street and Charlton Street, 20 August 1919.
Title page: Border Regiment, 1914.
Above: Visit of King George V and Queen Mary, June 1917.
Contents page: Border Regiment, 1914.
Back cover: 1st Tyneside Scottish Regiment, 1915.

Our grateful thanks to Brian Dalkin, Maureen Calcott, Ken Smith, Tyne & Wear Museums
& Archives, Sixtownships History Group, Newcastle Libraries Heritage Team and Anna
Flowers.

Contents

This book is dedicated to those who gave their lives and who were affected by 'The Great War'.

Postcard of War Memorial, Eldon Square, 1923.

Foreward

On 28 June 1914, Austrian Archduke Franz Ferdinand was assassinated by a Serbian nationalist. This incident placed additional stress on the already tense political situation in Europe, within months most of Europe and many other countries were at war. The conflict took place on land, at sea and in the air and claimed over 10 million lives.

Most of us have a mental picture of the First World War that is taken from silent films. It involves big guns, barbed wire and endless mud. The experience of war, however, was not confined to those who were fighting, but touched nearly every man, woman and child in the countries involved. For the first time in history war escaped the battlefield and found its way into the homes and workplaces of ordinary people on Tyneside and across Great Britain.

Vanessa Histon paints a picture of how global events affected the people of Tyneside, from 'Joining up' in 1914 through to the Armistice in 1918. The text and photographs are supported by the memories of two young women, Isabel Dalkin and Ruth Dodds, who were both in their mid-20s when war broke out in August 1914.

I acquired the diaries of Isabel Dalkin largely by chance. It was well known in the whole Dalkin family that Aunt Isabel, born in 1887, had kept diaries most of her adult life, but they had never been seen by anyone. Isabel died in November 1982 aged 95. I inherited the diaries when helping with the clearance of her flat in Gainsborough Grove, Fenham. We stuffed them into two biscuit tins that were pushed into the bottom of a wardrobe. Thirty years later I decided to take a look. The diaries ran from 1905 up to 1976, I transcribed the diaries from 1905 to 1916 including her comments on the First World War, some of which now appear in this book.

When walking around Newcastle today it is difficult to imagine the scenes of 100 years ago. With throngs of soldiers, mass parades and the general camaraderie of the population. However, Vanessa's narrative, archive photographs and personal accounts of the time, give a glimpse of what life was like on Tyneside during the Great War.

Brian Dalkin, April 2015.

Guards posted on King Edward VII Bridge, late 1914.

Joining up

When war was declared on 4 August 1914 the authorities were totally unprepared for the sheer numbers of men joining up throughout August and September. In his book *A Soldier's Life*, Thomas Hewitson reports that at one point there were 4,650 men in Newcastle's Fenham Barracks and a further 1,000 billeted with city families.

Thomas Hewitson quotes from the unpublished memoirs of Harry Fellows, who reported the chaos that greeted him when he arrived at Fenham Barracks in September 1914 to volunteer for the Northumberland Fusiliers:

… the barrack square was occupied by at least 2,000 men who were just sitting or walking about, each holding a blanket.

Asking for instructions from one of these men we were told to go and hand our papers in at a window on the far side of the square … [after which] we found ourselves the possessors of a blanket and then it was every man for himself. None of us had had anything to eat since breakfast but we could see there was no possible chance of us getting anything there.*

Harry and his friends (along with around 100 other volunteers, each with a blanket over their shoulder) decided to walk back to the Central Station, the only place in Newcastle that they knew. After a tip-off from a porter they spent the night in some empty railway coaches.

Arriving back at the barracks they discovered even greater chaos. More men had joined the recruits in the square and the pressure was on to find something from which to drink. Some men had acquired cups, mugs and even vases, but the local shops had already sold out of such items. When tea arrived in huge zinc baths there was a scramble to the cookhouse in search of empty food cans to use as cups. Some men were lucky but others had to wait until they could borrow something from another recruit.

After a meal consisting of a very thick hunk of bread and a spoonful of jam, the men continued to wander around until 3pm when the zinc baths returned, this time full of meat and vegetable stew. In the late evening, Harry was lined up with another 250 volunteers and marched to Tilly's Assembly Rooms. Finally he joined the 12th (Service) Battalion, the Northumberland Fusiliers.

On 5 August 1914, the day after war was declared, Ruth Dodds recorded:

Father went to Durham today in a carriage full of the 8th Durham Territorials. They got in at Chester-le-Street – pit hinnies all who had never obeyed any man's order, rowdy lads, with the pitman's bow-legged slouch to serve for marching, strong and short and ignorant but all in the highest spirits. The sergeant was a better educated man, who herded them in, but then let them hang out of the window shouting to their people. At last as the train moved, he shoved the lads into their places, and leaning out shouted 'Tak' care of the bairns!' to his own wife.

There was another civilian in the carriage. 'I suppose you're dying to meet a German?' he asked one of the lads. 'A German? By! If a meet a German A'm off!'

---

*Please note that throughout this book text from diaries, reports and newspapers has been reproduced as faithfully as possible, this may include spelling and language particular to the source text.

NORTHUMBERLAND ST. NEWCASTLE-ON-TYNE.

In Durham station Father saw a train with field-guns & munitions bound north.

Father can't think how the pitmen are ever to be drilled into shape; but they are better guarding the coasts than at home, for all the pits are laid idle.

The following day Isabel Dalkin and her fiancé Rankin Scoon had an evening drive through the centre of Newcastle. Isabel noted:

There are crowds of soldiers about. The Armstrong College & some of the hotels have been taken for hospitals. Some of the schools for the men to sleep in, while St James's Park & St Thomas's Church Yard are Military Encampments.

It soon became impossible to ignore the war. When they went to Tynemouth or Whitley Bay Isabel and Rankin saw soldiers defending the mouth of the Tyne or the coast, battleships, a submarine and searchlights. When they stayed in town they saw soldiers drilling. By the end of September, several of their friends had joined up.

On 14 August Ruth Dodds wrote:

Northumberland Street, 1914.

Father said he heard cavalry. We were all sitting in the breakfast-room after supper, there certainly was some rather faint cheering from the direction of the George IV [a public house]. I slipped on an old waterproof over my best dress & hurried out down the Lane … There was a convoy passing – endless it seemed, great waggons pulled by huge strong cart-horses, one after another. At first they were regulation waggons covered with karki [sic] tarpaulin, but by & by the square boxes [of ammunition?] were left quite naked on trolleys, & finally farm carts – anything that would do. They were not heavily laden to the eye, but two great horses pulled each, with a third at the tail, for hills, Father thought.

There was always a man driving & one walking with the leader & another with the tail horse, besides one or two walking beside. Between each cart was a mounted man, & officers rode up & down, shouting orders, which were generally 'halt' … It is very exciting to have seen a real convoy. They were all so hot & tired poor things, both men & horses.

There were all kinds of events aimed at encouraging men to volunteer for armed service. Many involved public meetings featuring motivating speeches, but a more imaginative venture was the military sports athletic festival, which opened on Newcastle's Town Moor on 31 July 1915 as part of a seven-week campaign aimed at inspiring 3,000 men to join up. In fact the forces gained 3,067 men as a result of Newcastle's efforts. Another novelty aimed at boosting recruitment was the exhibition of a German gun at the war memorial on Newcastle's Barras Bridge in December 1915. The gun, which had been captured from the battlefield at Loos, drew a large crowd, despite the wretched weather.

By September 1915 the number of men volunteering for armed service was beginning to dwindle. Heavy casualties at the front meant that more and more men were always needed so the Government, reluctant to introduce conscription before it was absolutely necessary, appointed the Earl of Derby as Director of Recruiting. In October 1915 he introduced a scheme to boost recruiting, under which men were asked to make an official commitment to serve and then await call up. It was understood that all single men would be called up before the youngest married man. Participants were given an armband to wear over their civilian clothes.

Isabel Dalkin's fiancé, Rankin Scoon, had applied for a Commission in the Royal Flying Corps in October 1915, but by December he was still waiting to hear whether or not his application had been successful. In the meantime he decided to join Lord Derby's scheme. He was accepted on 9 December.

Haymarket, October 1918. During 'Feed the Guns' week, guns and howitzers were arranged around the South African War Memorial.

Allied flags are suspended from the ceiling of the Cooperative Society's premises, now the Discovery Museum, where 'Kitchener's Recruits' awa their meal, 1916.

On 24 January 1916, Isabel wrote in her diary:

Rankin has had a letter from the War Office saying it will be advisable for him to go into the Machine Gun Section, so I don't know what he will do now.

On 28 January she recorded:

I see by the papers tonight that Rankin's group is to be called up shortly & as he has had no definite answer about the Flying Corps I really don't know what he will do. I will miss him horribly if he has to go away. I wish this dreadful war was all over.

Rankin went to London for a few days at the beginning of February and when he returned, Isabel had her answer:

I met Rankin at 11.15[pm] came home in a Taxi. He goes back tomorrow to join the Flying Corps.

Rankin had just 24 hours to prepare. On 9 February Isabel continued,

The train left at 11.19. Poor Rankin he did look awfully down hearted, guess I looked the same. How I will miss him. I wonder how long it will be before we meet again. He is going to sit an Exam in London tomorrow morning.

Lord Derby's scheme was not producing enough volunteers so the Military Service Act was passed in January 1916. It allowed for the conscription of single men aged under 41. The conscription of married men followed.

Conscription created genuine hardship for certain groups of men, including those who single-handedly had to care for sick or disabled family members and those trying to run businesses.

Appeals against conscription were heard by tribunals, but the majority were turned down. Often the exemptions that were granted were only temporary – just long enough for the individuals or businesses concerned to find someone else to take over the conscript's duties.

A number of cases were reported in the *Newcastle Journal*.

On 29 November 1916, readers were probably alarmed to discover that:

'A hearse is not a national necessity,' which was Judge Greenwell's comment on the case of a Tow Law undertaker, aged 29 and married. It was explained by Mr Robert Burrell for the appellant, that the applicant had 14 dependents. He was responsible for a hundred funerals annually, and had the only hearse between Crook and Consett.

Judge Greenwell then remarked that a hearse was not a national necessity, and Mr Burrell replied: 'The burial of the dead is.'

'But', added the Chairman, 'he would be much better employed in putting Germans into their coffins than carrying on this business.'

Mr Burrell: 'But in the mean time the people die and have to be buried.' The appeal was disallowed.

On 6 December *Journal* readers discovered that:

Two months' exemption was given to a manufacturing confectioner, aged 34, who had two sleeping partners. He had three brothers fighting. The appellant, who said the turnover was £25,000 a year, produced a tin of black bullets … and suggested that the members of the Tribunal should sample them. 'These are not the bullets wanted at the Front,' said Mr Renwick, and the man replied, 'Oh, yes; these are liked by our men, and scarcely anyone sends a parcel to the Front who does not send bullets or sweets of some kind.

Allied flags are suspended from the ceiling of the Cooperative Society's premises, now the Discovery Museum, where 'Kitchener's Recruits' await thier meal, 1916.

Employers were allowed to appeal on behalf of their workers and were expected to prove that no one else (not even a woman) could do the job in question. This could lead to derogatory statements about the capabilities of women.

A firm of dry cleaners applied for exemptions for three workers. When asked why their jobs couldn't be done by women, the firm's representative replied, 'I don't think there is a woman in the kingdom who can clean khaki suits. Women are not reliable for the work; they need such a lot of looking after.'

This seems astonishing as most housewives coped with cleaning their husbands' and families' clothes as a matter of course and tackling difficult stains like engine oil and coal dust would be part of the routine. Nevertheless, two of the dry cleaners were given exemptions of two months and the other received one month.

There were some young men who, for religious, political or other reasons, could not accept the idea of killing another human being. They were known as conscientious objectors and their cases were heard by military tribunals. At a time when so many men were being killed or wounded at the front, it was easy to dismiss their scruples as cowardice, so the 'conchies' were often treated harshly.

One of them was Scotswood-born poet, Basil Bunting, who had been educated in pacifist Quaker schools. In his biography *Basil Bunting: a Northern Life*, Anthony Flowers describes Bunting's tribunal. The 18-year-old told the tribunal that he objected to war and to non-combatant service (an alternative to fighting, such as being a stretcher bearer on the battle field or doing farm work at home, which could be offered to conscientious objectors, but was often rejected because it simply released another man for active service). He was prepared to let the 'German hordes' overrun England and would rather stay at home and let other men die for him in France.

'You are a beauty, you are!' replied the chairman of the tribunal.

Eventually Bunting was given a month to take up agricultural work or become a soldier. He did neither and was imprisoned, initially at Fenham Barracks and then at Wormwood Scrubs.

Isabel was right to worry about her fiancé, Rankin Scoon. By March 1916 he was in the Royal Flying Corp based in Bristol. On 28 March:

Got a letter from Rankin this morning then a card at dinner time to say they had had an accident at Castle Donnington as they were flying on to York, but he says he is alright so that is something to be thankful for. At 5.0 came a telegram asking me to send him some money so I sent £3. [The next day] Was pleased to get a letter from Rankin again to-day, he says he cut his nose in the accident. Something had gone wrong with the engine when 4,000 ft up and in planing (gliding?) down had hit a hedge and smashed the machine up a good deal.

This photograph shows Rankin Scoon's aircraft following his crash landing at Castle Donnington on on 28 March 1916. (Brian Dalkin).

Women at work

Working outside the home was a necessity for many women before the outbreak of war. They were employed in a huge variety of roles including factory workers, shop assistants, hairdressers, office workers, teachers and, of course, domestic servants. During the conflict, however, women were needed to work in what had been traditionally all-male preserves and they did it very successfully.

Almost as soon as war was declared, the Government came under pressure from women to create a uniformed service for them. The War Office soon realised the sense of this after an investigation showed that many jobs being done by soldiers in France could easily be taken over by women, freeing the men for combat.

The Women's Army Auxiliary Corps (WAAC) was established in December 1916 and renamed Queen Mary's Army Auxiliary Corps in April 1918. The Women's Royal Naval Service was formed in November 1917 and the Women's Royal Air Force was set up on 1 April 1918. In total, over 100,000 women joined up, doing jobs like administration and driving.

The armed forces needed nurses to care for both casualties overseas and those requiring convalescence or specialist treatment (during the First World War this involved the victims of shell shock) in the UK. Of course the civilian population continued to fall ill and have accidents just as they always had, so the recruitment of nurses became a priority.

Nursing had always been a job for women, but traditionally was considered unsuitable for those from middle and upper class backgrounds who had been sheltered from the troubling sights, sounds and smells and the hard work, long hours and strict discipline that hospital work involved.

Members of the Newcastle section of the Church Nursing and Ambulance Brigade. Top: 1918. Above: Summer Camp at Blagdon, July 1919.

Worried parents feared that a job that involved close personal contact with men would have a damaging effect on their daughters' reputations.

Still, women in their thousands volunteered as nurses (Voluntary Aid Detatchments or VADs) throughout the conflict. They provided field nursing services, mainly in hospitals, in the United Kingdom and overseas, and the majority of them were from the middle and upper classes.

On 13 March, 1916, Isabel Dalkin recorded:

Laura Heads is training to be a nurse she is going to the VAD Hospital at Etherly.

This was the 17th Durham VA Hospital at The Red House, Etherley, Bishop Auckland. Laura was 32 years old.

Ruth Dodds also had a friend who was a VAD. From the description of her working and living conditions she seems to have been deployed to a field hospital.

Above: Members of the Newcastle section of the Church Nursing and Ambulance Brigade.

On 22 December 1914 Ruth wrote:

Myra says the men are just splendid & laugh & joke when they are 'all to bits' & never grumble. The VAD live in two cattle trucks on a siding. She describes trying to feed 400 hungry men on bread & butter & tea with only one small spirit stove! … 'They inspect our bedrooms at 9.00 a.m. every morning (or say they do) & play around with our collars & waistbands as if we were 13 instead of all over 30 & many over 40 & put up notices to the effect that the credit of the detachment depends on the use of the clothes brush. You may form some idea of what we are putting up with 'pro patria [for our home land]' … once we have had a sight of our men return as they do, we [would] sell our souls & give our bodies to be burned for the sake of giving them half a glass of milk, so if Mrs F. or the CO [Commanding Officer] choose to inspect our toenails or make us repeat a hymn before retiring for the night we shall do it. But my God! It isn't as if they hadn't enough to do with the things that matter, e.g. store & food without waist-belt parades & clothes brush drill.' She is 12 hours on duty & 12 hours off & finds it difficult to get enough sleep.

In the North East, as elsewhere, buildings of all types were requisitioned as hospitals and a wounded serviceman could easily find himself being treated in a stately home, a hotel, a workhouse, or even Armstrong College (now Newcastle University). Isabel Dalkin wrote on 8 March 1916:

Herbert called at 7.00 he expects to go to Dilston Hall at Corbridge where he will be a convalescent patient, poor boy he does look so very delicate.

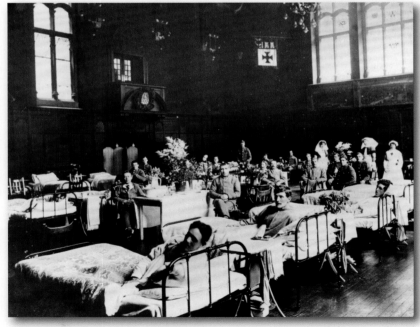

King's Hall, Armstrong College (now the University of Newcastle) was used as the First Northern General Hospital for Naval and Military Patients (Norman McCord).

1ST N.G. HOSPITAL. ARMSTRONG COLLEGE
WARD C.I.

Munitions work was relatively well paid – particularly when compared with the wages for domestic service, but it required 12-hour day or night shifts in unpleasant, dangerous conditions. Overtime could extend the working day to as much as 20 hours. Women filling shells worked with TNT, a poisonous explosive that could turn the skin yellow through toxic jaundice, a potentially fatal condition that earned the munitionettes, as they became known, the nickname 'canaries'. There was also the very real risk of being killed or maimed in an explosion.

In her article 'Arms and the Woman: Women and the War Industries on Tyneside 1914-1918' (*North East History* 2010), Maureen Calcott quotes Gladys Craig, aged 16 when war broke out, who recorded her memories for Beamish Museum:

… the wages were fantastic with time off as well … and I made plenty of money … making shells. I used to turn 100 a night. You were on a bonus if you could do that many. It was hard work and as you turned the steel off the shell it used to jump off in bits and I can tell you my body is tattooed with scars from doing that.

In October 1915, Newcastle started to encourage women from the 'educated classes' to volunteer for shell making at weekends to keep the machines going around the clock. One of these was Ruth Dodds, who wrote in her diary on 2 October 1915:

… hope I shall not find the work at Armstrong's … dull. However that will only be once a week at oftenest. I am very much excited over the scheme … Sylvie & I went to Fenwick's to see the munitions overalls. They are both pretty & useful.

The uniforms were worn with a fetching cotton cap, which was essential health and safety equipment as one woman found to her cost. Margaret Parker had only been working at Armstrongs for two nights:

…when I bent down and got my hair caught in a machine, and all pulled out … they sent us home, a bitter cold February morning and I had to walk home … I'd taken my hat off too soon, I was supposed to wear it, so I didn't get compensation or anything. [Maureen Calcott, 'Arms and the Woman'].

By 13 October, Ruth had finished her training and was a fully-fledged factory girl. She had also made a new friend, 20-year-old Annie Peacock who had been working at Armstrongs for four years (so she had started well before the outbreak of war).

[Annie] says it is terribly hard on night shift; the girls take it alternate weeks the hours are seven to seven; twelve hours out of twenty-four in the great gloomy echoing shops, where the artificial lights are always on & the rushing of the machinery never stops.

Outside the sunlight falls & the winds play on the river, but at this time of year the girls can hardly even see the sun once a day, for they go to work in the morning fog, & dark has fallen long before they come out.

Ruth described the younger girls as 'full of talk & fun' but worried about the older, married women 'with big families & the dinner & the washing always on their minds. You don't see them smile so often but even they haven't forgotten how.'

Annie told Ruth that Armstrongs employed 250 girls before the war, but by October 1915 this had risen to 8,700. This number increased as the war progressed.

Left: Ward C1, 1st Northern General Hospital during the First World War was housed in what is now the Hatton Gallery (TWAM and Robinson Library, Newcastle University).

While thousands of women were directly involved in caring for and supplying the troops, as more and more men joined the armed forces women's work became essential simply to keep everyday life in Britain running as smoothly as possible. It was during the war that women were first allowed to join the police force. Their main role was to maintain discipline and monitor women's behaviour around factories or hostels and make sure that women did not take anything into the factories that might cause explosions. They also worked with male officers, patrolling railway stations, streets, parks and public houses. From early 1917, women could join the Women's Land Army and play a vital part in keeping the nation supplied with food. Women took over their husbands' businesses. They delivered mail, worked on the railways and on the tramcars.

On 6 May 1915, the *North Mail* reported, with more than a hint of excitement at the novelty of the thing:

The arrival of the lady on the after-deck of the Newcastle tramcar has been awaited with interest, and her materialisation was noticed by a few observant persons in the city yesterday.

Fourteen trainee conductresses had been riding round the city in a tramcar all to themselves as they took it in turns to issue dummy tickets and imaginary change to their colleagues. Previously, 'on the derelict body of a

Women work in the Iron Foundry Department, Wallsend Slipway (TWAM).

motorless car,' they had been trained to push the bell and ensure that the tram stopped for passengers wishing to get on and off.

Their employers had been delighted, and somewhat surprised, that the women had learned the job so quickly. One official told the reporter:

A male is given 12 days to pick up his duties. It was the intention to give the women 14, but they are showing themselves such apt pupils that in every likelihood a briefer space of time will be enough to train them.

Two more groups of female trainees had already been selected. They would earn three shillings a day while training and sixpence an hour when they started work on the cars. Male beginners earned the same rates.

As soon as it was announced that the tramway committee was employing women, the offices were besieged with applicants. Over 400 women, from all walks of life, applied for 12 jobs as cleaners. The *North Mail* reporter was quick to emphasise that many of the women applying to work on the tramcars offered their services out of pure patriotism rather than economic necessity. They included a nurse, a governess, book keepers and other office workers, waitresses and shopkeepers and 'a lady who owns her own car'.

There were so many applicants that the tramway committee couldn't cope with them all so they were encouraged to use the women's war register at the labour exchanges.

A week later the *Journal* interviewed one of the female trainees, who was delighted to report that the work was light, the hours were satisfactory and the wages were munificent. She did worry, however, about what to do if faced with a passenger who was 'quarrelsome and inebriated'. She felt she

Above: Female workers meet George V and Queen Mary, Tyneside, June 1917.

Right: Female workers feed furnaces at Armstrong Whitworth and Company at Elswick. (© Imperial War Museum)

Female workers. Clockwise from top left: 1) The Wallsend Slipway and Engineering Company Limited, which constructed Mauretania's *turbines, 1914. (TWAM) 2) 'Apt pupils' – female conductresses sign up in 1915. 3) Female munitions workers at Armstrongs. 4) In new uniforms, 1914.*

wasn't up to throwing him off the tram himself so would leave this job to the driver.

Her male colleague told the reporter that as long as the women had the same pay and conditions as men his trade union principles would be safeguarded. He thought that the innovation would encourage more young men to enlist.

The 'average passenger' commented that the employment of conductresses didn't matter to him one way or the other. It would not affect any of the trials and tribulations faced by tram passengers so 'provided the lady conductor didn't give him his change in threepenny-pieces', he would accept her as part of his daily round.

On 19 May 1915 a meeting of women organised by the Newcastle Branch of the Catholic Women's League was held at the Town Hall, Newcastle.

On the following day, the *Evening Chronicle* reported:

The Lord Mayor, who chaired the meeting said that the men of Newcastle had responded nobly to the call of their King and country. The women had also responded and were still responding, and he trusted that they would continue to respond until the present terrible conflict had been brought to a successful and victorious conclusion. More men and still more men were required and munitions also …

The Corporation of Newcastle had set a very good example for they had released several hundred tram conductors, and women were taking their places. The women were being paid at the rate of 6d per hour. Several thousands of women were working at Messrs. Armstrongs to release men. The gravity of the situation had not yet been brought home to some. It must be remembered we were fighting unscrupulous and dangerous foes, and they must be crushed and beaten at whatever cost.

In February 1917, courageous conductress Mrs Eva Barrass was recognised for her bravery when she was presented with money collected after a public appeal. Eva had been working on a Westgate Road Tram when she spotted a gang of pickpockets operating on the vehicle. She not only warned passengers to look out for their belongings but also helped to arrest the three culprits. She was complimented on the 'zealous manner … in which she had safeguarded the interests of West End citizens'. [*North Mail*, 9 February 1917]

Some women actually lost their jobs when war broke out and some businesses closed. The Women Workers' Committee decided to help former waitresses, dressmakers, shop girls and netmakers by training them to make toys. There were schemes in Newcastle and North Shields. It may seem a trivial choice of business for wartime, but until 1914 many popular toys, including the majority of dolls, sold in this country were made in Germany. On the outbreak of war toy imports ceased

Above: Women take up window cleaning in Newcastle, 1914.

immediately and it was considered a threat to morale to make children, many of whose fathers were fighting, do without playthings. Toy making enterprises were encouraged. Tyneside lasses did particularly well and, at an exhibition and sale of their work on Blackett Street on 19 December, 1914, it was said that their toys were equal to German craftsmanship, if not better.

Figures from the Labour Exchange revealed that sempstresses, dressmakers and tailoresses had been the most badly hit by the war and the Women's Employment Sub-Committee of the Lord Mayor's War Relief Committee had set up a number of schemes in Newcastle to help them. A workroom at 51 Northumberland Street employed 20 women to repair donated clothes for redistribution among the needy. Around the corner at 51 Blackett Street, there was an office that received orders for items needed by soldiers and sailors, which were placed with unemployed needlewomen. Between 80 and 100 women each week were helped in this way. The Sub-Committee also set up training in domestic work (including cookery, laundry work, household mending and sewing) for 'a certain number of selected unemployed girls'.

There was no conscription for women in the United Kingdom, but there were facilities for women to register their skills and their willingness to do voluntary work. Isabel Dalkin commented on 14 August, 1915:

Rankin is a bit in the dumps because I offered my services as a driver on the National Registration Papers.

She doesn't record whether her services were called upon much, but on 27 October 1915, she mentions:

Pa & I went out in the car at 9.30. I took him to the

Cow Hill Fair then brought the car down home. I spent the whole day cleaning it as I am going to take some wonderful soldiers up to Mrs Kendals for tea tomorrow.

[The next day] *It has been a horrible wet day so my clean car was all lashed up. Went down to the College* [presumably Armstrong College, which had been converted into a hospital] *about 2.30. Brought 2 loads of soldiers up* [to Mrs Kendal's]*. Had a lovely tea & a fine sing song. Poor boys. It makes my heart ache to see them. Took 3 loads back at night.*

Driving was much in demand. Advertisements encouraging parents to consider driving lessons for girls appeared in Theatre Royal programmes in 1918: ' … so your daughter can do work of national importance. Employment is assured – it is a post-war profession'. People were starting to realise that the staggering loss of young men during the conflict meant that many women would have no chance of marriage and be obliged to earn their own livings.

Volunteers did all kinds of much-needed tasks from staffing refreshment carts and canteens, not just for soldiers and sailors, but for female workers too, to rolling bandages. One local newspaper published instructions for making gas masks from triangular bandages and cotton pads soaked in bicarbonate of soda that could easily be made by volunteers and were issued to troops facing poison gas attacks from 1915.

Volunteers were also required to sit on the many committees that organised the work of other volunteers.

Another vital skill during wartime was knitting. Everyone who could knit was encouraged to spend their spare time producing basic clothing for the forces. On 5 November 1914, Isabel Dalkin notes:

I shall have to start to do some knitting for the poor soldiers they are asking in all the papers for socks, pullovers, etc.

An undated local newspaper cutting describing the sale of unclaimed property left behind on tramcars commented: 'Bundles of knitted socks were numerous this year, due no doubt to the war'. As well as knitting as a patriotic duty, women tried to supply family, friends and even strangers in the forces with some of the comforts of home. Isabel Dalkin often mentions sending parcels of homemade scones and cake to her brother Joe and cigarettes to other friends. Meanwhile Ruth Dodds and her family were sending parcels to two soldiers, at least one of whom was a stranger. They sent 'a great number of little things' that included tobacco and cigarettes to be shared with other soldiers. The Dodds family also sent parcels to a prisoner of war in Germany and on 1 October 1915 Ruth wrote:

We have heard from our prisoner in Germany & he likes our parcels, especially food, & he writes a good hand & no one else is sending him anything. Today in town we bought him books, (which he specially asked for) good long stodgy old-fashioned ones like The Moonstone & Nicholas Nickelby & The Golden Butterfly.

Women begin driving for Armstrong-Whitworth works.

Women's involvement in war work was recognised and celebrated, and is usually held to be a contributing factor in the granting of the vote in 1918 to women aged over 30. However as soon as men came back from the war, most women were abruptly dismissed. One of them was Bertha Elliot, who had spent the war in the luxurious surroundings of Coxon's department store (on the corner of Grey Street and Market Street) where she thoroughly enjoyed selling gloves to wealthy and elegant ladies. She was surprised and delighted to get a 'little bit of money from the dole'. Meanwhile there was a national scandal about the number of men who had been prepared to die for their country who returned from the war to discover that country could not even offer them employment.

Above: Armstrongs munitions workers pose for the camera.
Right: A female ticket collector on a tram at Osborne Road, 1916 (John Airey)

Zeppelins

In 1915 and 1916, the Germans brought the war right to the doorsteps of ordinary British citizens for the very first time. They used airships called Zeppelins to bomb towns and cities near the east coast. Tyneside, with its shipbuilding and other industries, was a prime target.

Zeppelin raids caught the Government completely by surprise. They anticipated and prepared for attack by sea, but no one imagined that death and destruction would come from the air. To make matters worse, Zeppelins could cut their engines at 11,000 feet and drift silently towards their target. There was no warning.

The Government and local authorities worked together to devise a list of measures that would save lives and minimise damage to property in the event of bombing raids or, even worse, invasion by air. Newcastle residents were requested to dim lights 'as far as reasonably practicable' and if a raid did occur to extinguish any lights that showed outside immediately. People were advised to go, or stay, inside, preferably in cellars or the lower parts of buildings.

In the event of an invasion people were advised not to leave as 'all necessary steps have been taken by the military authorities to defend the city'. Arrangements were in place for the evacuation of the city should it become necessary, but cars and other vehicles would not be allowed to leave before permission was given.

On 28 February 1915, Isabel Dalkin wrote:

The town looks funny now a days, there are so few lights on, all the tops of the lamps have been darkened in case there should be an air raid.

On 14 April, she thought the air raid precautions were having some effect:

There was a Zeppelin raid tonight, the town was in darkness and the car stopped, very little damage was done with the bombs.

It is possible that Isabel didn't realise exactly how widespread the raid was. The *Journal* of 15 April carried reports from all over the region.

At around 8pm an airship approached Blyth from the coast, where it was engaged with rifle fire by the 1st Battalion of Northern Cyclists. It hovered over the marketplace where a large crowd was attending a recruiting meeting (it's interesting to speculate how many young men were inspired to join up by the outrageous appearance of the enemy in their home town) before flying on to Choppington, dropping five bombs and breaking windows but causing no other damage. There were also reports of bombs at Seaton Delaval and Bedlington, where a man was injured when debris struck his hand and someone else helpfully picked up an unexploded bomb and carried it to the police station!

Six bombs were dropped on Wallsend at around 8.40. An incendiary bomb crashed through the roof of a house on Station Road, falling through the ceiling and injuring an old lady who had been sitting by the kitchen fire. The furniture in the bedroom was scattered about by the blast. Three bombs fell on the railway station, two of them directly in front of a stationary electric train. Although the sleepers caught fire the 'timely arrival of the fire brigade prevented serious damage.' Another bomb landed in the river near a 'well-known shipyard'. There were also reports of two bombs landing in a shipyard at Hebburn.

Bombs were reported at Benton, 'where the military have been making trenches west of Benton Churchyard', and the area known as 'the White City' where a cyclist had his bike smashed and one of his eyes injured by a splinter. At Dudley the windows were blown out of the Post Office and a bomb fell into the garden at Seaton Burn House without causing any damage. Annitsford and Killingworth were also bombed.

Although there were no bombs reported at North Shields and the electric lighting was turned on again at 10.55, the town's authorities decided not to restore the gas supply until 10am the following day.

The *Journal* was full of praise for Tynesiders who behaved with 'commendable coolness. On no hand was there any sign of fear or panic. The prevailing feeling was chiefly one of intense curiosity'.

The real problem involved getting home. The raid took place on a Wednesday, half-day closing in the shops, so people had flocked to the towns, especially Newcastle, for a night out. The streets were so dark that people could not find their way around, the tramcars came to a sudden stop and all the taxis had been commandeered by the military authorities. Most train services had been suspended and no one knew when they would start again. In Newcastle people rushed to the Central Station, only to be turned away by the police who were worried about the potential loss of life if the station was hit by a bomb.

Air raid precautions continued and raids soon became a fact of life. There was bad news from the Front and Isabel Dalkin seemed to find the darkened city streets lowered her mood even further. On 27 April she wrote:

The streets are all in darkness now-a-days & no lights in the shop windows. Nearly all the boys who went out last weekend have been straight to the Front, a great many of them will never come back again.

On 6 May she recorded:

Everyone has got notice to have lights well shaded & windows covered at night & to have candles ready in case of emergency. There are 13,000 more men needed from the North. I'm afraid it will mean conscription soon.

That emergency arrived on 15 June. Isabel notes:

We were rather alarmed at 11.15 by seeing flames in the sky & hearing loud reports from guns then there was a large fire in the East. We afterwards learned it was a Zepplin [sic] which set fire to some of Palmers Workshops, wrecked some homes & killed about 20 people.

Air raids held an awful fascination for some people, including Isabel and her family. On 16 June she wrote:

Willie, mother, Rankin, Harry & I had a run out in the car at night to see some of the carnage from the bombs at Wallsend there are hundreds of windows shattered.

Attacks from the air threatened life and property, but they also disrupted people's lives and lowered their morale. On 10 February 1916 Isabel wrote:

At 6.00 mother & I went down to the Grey St Picture House. Sat there for 20 mins, when out went all the lights. The Theatre was then emptied as it was reported that Zeps had been sighted near the coast. Mother & I walked home. The lights were turned on again at 9.00.

A 'Zeppelin-eye' view of Newcastle, 1917. (TWAM)

More seriously, Ruth Dodds, a part-time munitionette at Armstrongs, recorded a colleague's experiences in the factory:

One night last winter about eleven o'clock [halfway through a twelve-hour shift] all the lights went out; the buzza had sounded three times, which mean they were turned off on purpose. For four & a half hours those two thousand girls waited in the dark, expecting Zeppelin bombs any moment. It was bitterly cold with the lights off, some screamed & some fainted, & some sang in chorus & some to themselves, & presently some lighted up their gases & heated up their tea on them. As for Annie, she went into the next shop among the older girls & had a good sleep.

As the air raids continued they became something of a distraction for Isabel Dalkin, and she records several occasions when she either watched raids in progress or went to see the damage they had caused.

On 2 April 1916:

There was a raid last night we were watching the flashes of the bombs from our window. I had to take the car out in the afternoon [as] Pa called at some farms near Boldon so we went on to Sunderland to see the damage which the Zeps had done.

The next day:

There was another Air Raid last night about 11.30. We were watching the bombs dropping this time the Zeps were near Ponteland & Gosforth.

On 8 April Isabel wrote:

Madge & I went for a ride in the afternoon along the Stamfordham Rd. We saw the holes in the fields that the bombs from the Zeps had made.

Above: A Schutte Lanz Zeppelin caught in search lights near Elwick in an air raid on Hartlepool just before midnight on 27 November 1916. Zeppelins were difficult to shoot down because they could fly higher and climb faster that a lot of aircraft, they could also remain aloft even when holed. (Hartlepool Libraries)

The Newcastle Committee published special instructions to citizens in the *Journal* on 29 January 1915. The Lord Mayor of Newcastle (Alderman John Fitzgerald) issued a notice to forewarn residents of impending danger and reassurance that the authorities had put plans and measures in place to protect the population:

1)   Although no new or special grounds for apprehension exist at present, I desire it to be known that an Emergency Committee formed by the military authorities has been making arrangements that are considered necessary, in the event of an emergency arising, in order to facilitate the operations of His Majesty's Forces, to hinder those of the enemy, and to safeguard the civil population.

2)   Residents in the City are requested to diminish open lights as far as reasonably practicable, and, in the case of an actual air raid, to extinguish immediately all light which show externally. The civil population should, in the case of an air raids, go, or remain indoors, preferably in the lower parts of the building or its cellars.

3)   In the event of an air raid involving the landing of the enemy in the neighbourhood of the City, residents are advised not to leave, as all necessary steps have been taken by the military authorities to defend the City.

4)   In the event of an invasion involving an attack in force upon the City, arrangements have been made, and directions will be given for the movement of such of the civil population as desire to leave, and for the placing of all transport vehicles under the control of the military authorities and the Emergency Committee. In the event of such and emergency, no motor cars or other vehicles will be allowed to leave the City before permission is given. Provision has also been made, of the occasions should arise, for the removal or destructions of material which might be of assistance to the enemy.

5)   It is hoped that in any emergency the people of Newcastle Upon Tyne will preserve a calm demeanour, and will follow the instructions given to them by police, special constables or others in authority.

Top: A 1915 photo 'montage' postcard showing a Zeppelin over Blyth. (Sixtownships History Group)

Above: Damage to a building at Cramlington following the Zeppelin Raid on April 14, 1915.

ZEPPELIN RAID, APRIL 14th, 1915.

On 14 April 1915 the German Naval Zeppelin, L9 visited Tyneside. After the event residents of Cramlington gathered around the craters left by the bombs, some craters had a circumferance of 60 feet. Top right: Remains of the bombs were collected by local people. (Above images courtesy of Sixtownships History Group)

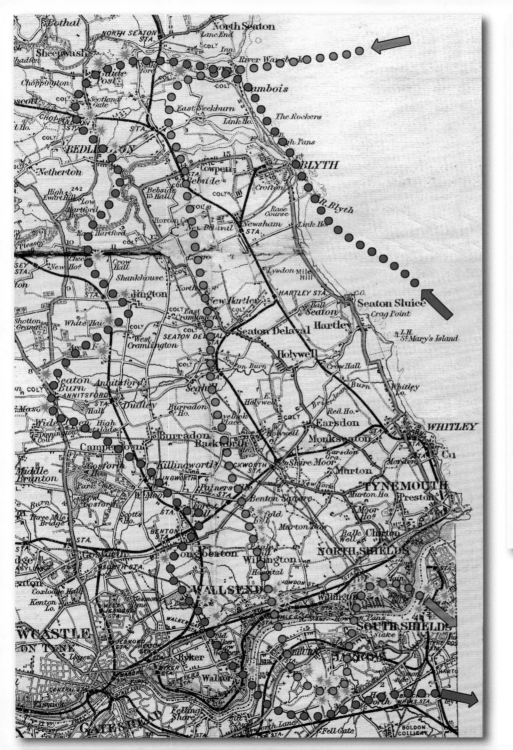

Zeppelin L9

14 April 1915.

Reached British coast at Blyth at 7.30.

Left British coast at 9.00 south of Marsden.

Weather: Little wind on the NE Coast, slight mist and rain over mouth of Tyne.

Total number of bombs dropped: 31

Killed: 0

Injured: 2

Damage: £55

Zeppelin L10

15 June 1915.

Reached British coast near Cambois at 11.25.

Left British Coast at 11.52 over South Sheilds.

Weather: Moderate wind on NE coast. Fine, Clear Sky.

Total number of bombs dropped: 53

Killed: 18

Injured: 72

Damage: £41,760

A map showing two of the Zeppelin attacks. The route of the Zeppelins and the bomb sites are approximate.

Adapted from a map published in The War in the Air: Being the story of the part played in the Great War by the Royal Air Force *by Sir Walter A. Raleigh and Henry A. Jones, 1922.*

On 9 August Isabel wrote:

There was an Air Raid at Whitley [Bay] last night, so Madge, Flora & I cycled down there after an early tea. Some of the houses are badly damaged & a tremendous lot of glass has been broken, mostly near the Station. After we had a look around we went to the Band on the Links for a short while then left for home at 8.15 [and] had a fine run back.

For others, their first sight of a Zeppelin was truly terrifying:

My mother, who was born in Heaton, told me that she remembered being taken as a little girl in around 1916, (so she'd have been six or seven), into the street by their housemaid to see a Zeppelin passing overhead. This was presumably in daylight. She said it was very frightening and she never forgot the sight. It seemed enormous to her, and very sinister. I'm not sure if there was an accompanying sound. Perhaps the Zeppelin was on its way to bomb somewhere. (Anna Flowers).

By the end of May 1916 at least 550 British civilians had been killed by German Zeppelins, despite the Government doing its best to counter the threat. Observers and searchlights were mobilised in an attempt to give early warnings of attack. Artillery guns were used to attack Zeppelins, but they weren't particularly effective as the airships could fly beyond their reach. However, by 1916 Britain was using fighter planes and specially developed incendiary ammunition to pierce the shells of the Zeppelins. This ignited the gas used to keep the airships afloat and they fell to the ground. In this way 77 of Germany's fleet of 115 Zeppelins were destroyed or damaged beyond repair. This was too high a cost for Germany and soon the number of Zeppelin raids started to dwindle.

Tyne industries at war

As a major centre for engineering and heavy industry, Tyneside played a crucial role in producing the hardware of war including guns, munitions, ships, aeroplanes and airships.

Armstrong's industrial empire was responsible for the production of 13,000 guns, 14 million shells and 100 pioneering tanks as well as warships.

In 1913 Armstrong-Whitworth took over a disused skating rink on the north side of Grandstand Road in Gosforth. It was used as an aircraft factory throughout the war, producing planes such as the BE2c, and, towards the end of the war, the Bristol F2B fighter. During the conflict a total of 1,275 aeroplanes and three rigid ships were flown off from the Duke's Moor.

Maritime historian Ken Smith has researched the role of the Tyne's shipyards and ship repair yards during the conflict. The river's shipyards were working at full stretch to produce warships and Ken discovered that Swan Hunter & Wigham Richardson completed 55 vessels for the admiralty including: 'two cruisers, 28 torpedo-boat destroyers, a monitor (heavy gun ship), five submarines, seven sloops, two Q-ships (armed vessels disguised as peaceful merchant ships), seven convoy sloops, one troopship, one repair and depot ship and one hospital ship'. Swan's award winning luxury liner, *Mauritania*, completed in 1907, served as a troop and hospital ship during the conflict. Meanwhile Hebburn's Hawthorn

Clockwise from top left: 1) In 1913 Armstrong-Whitworth took over a skating rink on the Town Moor near Grandstand Road, here BE2c aircraft being built. 2) Female workers in the shell shop at the Neptune Shipyard of Swan Hunter and Wigham Richardson Ltd, October 1917. (TWAM) 3) After a cycling trip to Whitley Bay on 5 August, 1916, Isabel Dalkin records that she 'came round by the Grand Stand where we had a good look at an aeroplane'.

A rail-mounted 12 inch Mark 9 gun at Armstrongs works 1916. This gun weighed 152 tons and could throw a 850 pound shell 33,000 yards.

King George V surveys the shipyard of John Readhead & Sons Ltd, South Shields during his visit to the North East coast, 16 June 1917. (TWAM)

German submarine UB 110 was built by Blohm & Voss, Hamburg. On 19 July 1918 she attacked a convoy of merchant ships near Hartlepool, she was depth-charged by HM Motor-Launch No.263 and then rammed by HMS Garry before sinking. She was salvaged and taken to Swan Hunter's with a view to restoring her, however the armistice ended restoration work and on 19 December 1918 was sold as scrap and towed to Northumberland Dock. (TWAM)

Leslie produced 30 ships for the Royal Navy and Readhead's of South Shields built 26.

The damage sustained by ships during the conflict kept the ship repair yards busy too, with Swan's alone repairing 556 vessels including 249 warships.

Swan's was also involved in producing armaments: at the Neptune Yard in Low Walker women forged more than 270,000 six-inch shells and completed nearly 100,000 of them ready for filling.

One of Armstrong's warships had a rather chequered history. Ordered in 1910 by Brazil, the *Rio de Janeiro* (as she was then called) could not be delivered because the Brazilian government ran out of money to pay for her. She was then bought by Turkey and ordered to be renamed *Sultan Osman I*. A Turkish crew came over to Newcastle to take delivery of the ship, but went home empty handed as, with the country on the verge of war, the British Government had seized her. Renamed HMS *Agincourt*, she fought at the Battle of Jutland in 1916.

Another of Armstrong's pioneering vessels was the aircraft carrier HMS *Furious*. She carried a Sopwith Camel, which raided German Zeppelin airship hangars in 1918.

Living from day to day

The demands of war had an effect on almost every aspect of daily life.

Even children's schooling was disrupted. The log book of Todd's Nook School records on 25 August 1914: 'On account of War with Germany only morning school is being held. The infants from Wingrove School are occupying this department in the afternoons, as their school is in the hands of the Military Authorities.'

Many mothers were working and although some official childcare was provided it was simply not enough. Some children were left to survive on the streets outside school hours, with older children looking after their younger siblings.

Potential food shortages and rising prices were a concern right from the outbreak of war. On 8 August 1914, the *Journal* reported:

Though the grocery and provision establishments in Newcastle and district are still experiencing a busy time, the rush which was in evidence in the early part of the week had largely subsided yesterday. Some firms were compelled to keep closed in order to deal with the large number of orders they had received by telephone and post, but most of the shops remained open as usual. No important changes took place in retail prices during the day, and now that the public has got into a more reasonable frame of mind, the probability is that for several classes of commodities the charges will go down somewhat. This will certainly be the case with flour.

The *Journal* went on to reassure readers that there was no shortage of wheat – an 'exceptional' harvest would be supplemented by imports from Canada. The recent problem with flour supplies had been caused by a combination of panic buying and the fact that so many horses and vehicles had been requisitioned by the army that there were 'temporary' problems with transport. The Newcastle Co-operative stores had reported that the only item that had risen in price was butter, which was 1d per pound dearer than it had been the previous week. However the store had introduced its own rationing system for members.

Top: A busy Grainger Street, 1917. Bottom right: A colour postcard of Grey Street, showing the Theatre Royal and Grey's Monument, 1910s. Bottom left: A postcard of Fenwick's on Northumberland Street, 1914.

Perhaps the *Journal*'s calming words were over confident because on 10 August 1914 the paper reported:

Regrettable scenes were witnessed at Benwell on Saturday night, where a large crowd, incensed, it is stated, by the rise that had been made in the price of provisions, attacked a certain shop, and vented their anger by smashing the windows and scattering the goods within. Afterwards they did damage to other similar establishments.

The police were called to the scene, and the crowd were soon dispersed. No personal injuries appear to have been done.

More 'regrettable scenes' could be witnessed at German pork butchers' shops, which had been very popular before the war for their cooked meats, pies, sausages and saveloys. As soon as the hostilities started, eating German food was considered unpatriotic and anyone with a German-sounding name was suspect. On Tyneside and elsewhere German butchers' shops were attacked and damaged by angry crowds. German and Austrian men who had not become British citizens were interred and their wives and families deported to their country of origin, where they were bullied because they were viewed as British sympathisers.

German U-boat attacks on allied merchant shipping, and the fact that many of the men and horses that had worked in agriculture were on military service, eventually led to grave food shortages and there were long queues at grocers' shops. In 1916 British Summer Time was introduced to give farmers and others more daylight hours in which to work.

Meat rationing was introduced in 1918 and the Lord Mayor of Newcastle explained to the *Journal* on 23 January:

The working men of Newcastle … are quite ready to tighten their belts and do their best under the circumstances, if they can be assured that they receive a fair share of the food. There are thousands of working men doing very hard manual work, men who are not able to have meat dinners, and who return from work too late at night for a substantial meal. They, I think should have the first claim on the bacon supply for their breakfast.

There was no mention of the thousands of working women who, after equally long shifts, also had to buy the food and cook it.

Newcastle introduced its own temporary meat rationing scheme in February 1918. The *Journal* reported on 22 February:

The new temporary rationing scheme for Newcastle was put to its fullest test yesterday, when housewives were in search of the week-end joint. On past Fridays the queues at butchers' shops were largest, but yesterday they were conspicuous by their absence. The customers seemed satisfied with the rapidity with which they were served, even if they were not quite pleased with the 1s 3d per head ration. The butchers were more than satisfied that the day of the queue has gone. A few queues were still to be seen at the pork butchers, and this was largely due to the fact that there was a marked scarcity of pork of all kinds. Indeed, even a small portion of such flesh for roasting purposes was not available. It was stated that scarcely a dozen pigs had reached the pork butchers in Newcastle to meet the week-end trade.

Later in the year Newcastle's temporary meat rationing scheme was replaced by a national scheme that allowed 2lb meat per head. Sugar, flour, butter, margarine and milk were also rationed and there were shortages of other essentials such as coal.

Drinking represented another huge problem for the government. As Lloyd George put it: 'Drink is doing more

Opposite: Rationing was introduced in February 1918 to control consumption of meat, sugar, flour, butter and milk. Cards were issued by the Food Controller. Top right: Confectioners on Chillingham Road, Heaton. Bottom right: Hugel's Butchers, Station Road, Newburn. The Hugels were imprisoned as enemy aliens and did not reopen the shop after the war. Centre: 'Regrettable scenes' were played out in Benwell, Adelaide Terrace, 1910s.

RETAILER'S SUGAR TICKET.

This Ticket is issued under the authority of the Food Controller by:—

(Retailer's Name and Address, written or rubber-stamped.)

Wm. STEWART & SON,

88, GRAINGER STREET,

NEWCASTLE.

NEWCASTLE UPON TYNE

Food Control Committee

This Card is issued under the Authority of the Food Controller to

Rev Wm B East

r/c

2

NOT TRANSFERABLE.

PLEASE KEEP THIS CARD CLEAN.

Local Food Office:

TOWN HALL

This card is the property of the Newcastle upon Tyne Food Control Committee, and must be delivered up to them at any time on demand.

Instructions.

Do not write upon or mark this Card in any way.

Take it to a shop within the City of Newcastle upon Tyne, on or before 18th April, 1918.

You may select one shop for each commodity (Butter or Margarine being treated as one).

The Shopkeeper will place his name in the spaces provided.

You must take this Card to the Shop every time you go to buy any of the articles named on the other side.

If you change your address, or if there is any change in the number of your household, report the alteration to the Executive Officer at the Local Food Office, Town Hall, Newcastle upon Tyne.

It is an offence under the Defence of the Realm Acts to transfer this card or to use it for any person not included in the number for whom it is issued, and the articles to which it refers must only be purchased from the Shopkeeper who registers your card.

GEORGE LUNN, Lord Mayor

* The registration of this card carries no guarantee of supplies.

ANDREW REID & COMPANY, LIMITED, NEWCASTLE-UPON-TYNE.

damage in the war than all the German submarines put together.'

Many people, especially women, had more disposable income than ever before, and that, combined with the stress of being at war and the anxiety of having a husband, sweetheart, son or brother at the front, often led people to the pub. Consequently some men, and more shockingly women, were turning up for work drunk, hungover or not at all. This could slow down production and, in the case of already dangerous jobs, such as mining, shipbuilding and munitions work, lead to devastating accidents.

The government's response included reducing the opening hours of pubs (in Newcastle pubs were required to close at 9pm instead of 11pm) and diluting the strength of spirits. New laws meant that landlords offering credit to pub customers, and people buying rounds or even treating a friend to a drink could be charged with criminal offences.

Fun and fundraising

Day-to-day life on the home front was undoubtedly hard, but there was always entertainment to be had. Many people had more money than ever before and they desperately needed to escape from the ugly reality of the war, so theatres, music halls, picture houses and dance halls were thriving. Isabel Dalkin usually went to the theatre or cinema every few days and her social life also included whist drives and dances.

Almost any event, whether professionally or privately organised, could be turned into an opportunity for charitable fundraising. Money was always needed for everything from buying tanks and guns to providing some support for the invalids, widows and orphans that they created.

Wartime programmes from Newcastle's Theatre Royal show that the theatre and its patrons provided an enormous amount of support for war charities. In 1915 alone it hosted a collection for Polish refugees, the chance to buy a souvenir 75mm gun and help the French, 'our Noble Allies', and presented a 'Grand Concert in Aid of the War Hospital Fund for Officers'. Charitable activities continued after the war, with, for example 'The stage's tribute to Blind Soldiers. The Compton Comedy Co. appearing in *The Importance of being Earnest*. The whole of the receipts to be handed over to Sir Arthur Pearson's fund', which was staged on 29 May 1919.

Sport was another morale booster, but with the majority of fit young men serving in the forces it was difficult to put a team together. The football league suspended all its matches after the 1914/15 season.

Once again it was women who filled the gap. Women workers in munitions factories started kicking a football around during their breaks. Employers and the Government encouraged this as a way of keeping workers fit and healthy. Gradually the munitionettes formed teams and played matches against injured soldiers and women's teams from other factories. The novelty of women playing football (and possibly the unaccustomed sight of female legs, albeit enclosed in thick long socks) drew big crowds and raised money for war charities.

Soon the women were appreciated for their skill instead of their novelty value. The undoubted star of North East women's football was Bella Reay, who played several times for Newcastle United Ladies at St James's Park and

Opposite: Clockwise from top left: 1) Clayton Street, The Newcastle Arms, 1910s. 2) A colour postcard of Northumberland Street, 1917. 3) Isabel Dalkin and friend. (Brian Dalkin). 4) 'The Black House' at the corner of Pilgrim Street and Worswick Street, 1918.

KITTY the Willington Quay DONKEY
Who has been the means of raising over £250 for Charities during the War.
ONE PENNY EACH.

Clockwise from top left: 1) War time advert, encouraging people to come to the King's Hall Cinema on Marlborough Crescent in Newcastle. 2) Newcastle Hoppings, Jesmond Vale 1914. 3) Children help out at Denton School, 1910s. 4) Kitty the donkey who raised over £250 for charities during the war with children collecting for the Belgian Relief Fund, circa 1915.

went on to play for England. Her main team, however, was Blyth Spartans Ladies FC, whose members had been taught to play by sailors on the beach. They were never defeated and won the Munitionettes Cup in 1918 in front of a crowd of 22,000. So dedicated were the Spartans players that one team member, Jennie Morgan, came straight from her wedding to play in a match and scored two goals. Bella herself scored 133 goals in one season.

When the war ended and the munitions factories closed many of the teams disbanded although a few continued to play. Far from encouraging women to keep fit by playing football, there was a tremendous backlash against the sport, even from female doctors like Dr Mary Scharlieb of Harley Street, who declared it the 'most unsuitable game, too much for a woman's physical frame'.

In December 1921, on the grounds of football's unsuitability for females, the FA banned women's football at their grounds. The ban effectively ended women's football in the UK until it was lifted in 1971.

Not exactly a social event, but a huge draw all the same, was the visit of Julian the Tank Bank to Newcastle. A number of tanks had been touring towns and cities in the UK to encourage people to invest in war bonds and Tank No. 113 (pet name Julian) arrived at Newcastle's Forth Goods Yard and was taken via Neville Street, Grainger Street and Northumberland Street to the Haymarket, where it stayed for the week of 31 December 1917.

According to the *Evening Chronicle* of 1 January, 1918, Julian had record takings of £680,225 on his first day, despite the persistent drizzle. The crowds that surrounded the tank were entertained by military bands and speeches on the wisdom of saving. Comparisons with the amount of money raised in Liverpool and Manchester spurred the Tynesiders on to invest (this was a sizeable commitment as war bonds cost a minimum of £5 and war savings certificates were 15s 6d each) and an element of local competition was introduced by giving each investor a coloured disc according to where they lived (red for Gateshead, blue for Jarrow and white for Wallsend), which they could fix to the side of the tank. Each day the local picture houses screened the amount subscribed. A further inducement was offered by the proprietors of Fenwick's department store who promised to give every twelfth buyer of certificates between certain hours another certificate free of charge. Fenwick's store closed for an hour on Friday to give staff the opportunity of investing.

The crowd at the Tank Bank also had the opportunity of seeing war hero Lance-Corporal John George Wells, RAMC, receive his Military Medal for saving the lives of members of a tank crew who had been shelled and gassed. The presentation took place on top of Julian. Another triumph for the Government's publicity machine was the announcement that anyone who wished to invest £100 or more but was unable to visit the Tank Bank in person could send in their application by specially trained carrier pigeon.

Despite the Government's best efforts, not everyone quite understood the purpose of the Tank Bank. The same *Evening Chronicle* report mentions:

An old man from outside the city [who] placed on the counter the sum of £500 and asked, 'What do you think of that for an offer for the tank?' He took some convincing that the Tank was not for sale.

Clockwise from top left: 1) These ladies find time to relax at the coast, note the cycles in the background, 1910s. 2) Cinema Palace, Benwell. 3) Jesmond Vale, Whit Monday Hoppings, 1914.

Clockwise from top left: 1) Westerhope Methodist Church Football Team, 1914. 2) Newcastle United's team 1914-1915. 3) Clayton Street, showing the Gaumont Cinema in 1915.

The Armistice and after

On 7 October 1918, Ruth Dodds recorded in her diary:

It was a Sunday afternoon that Uncle Eustace brought in a 'Mail' with the German peace offer. I was simply shaking with excitement, but I had enough self-control not to argue with him when he began to say that we must never sheath the sword while one brick of Berlin stood upon another & that sort of thing. It was terrible; I ran upstairs to pray but couldn't quiet my nerves ... Even if peace comes it comes too late – so many lives lost, so many hearts broken. None of the men of 'my lot' are alive now, I think. But there are still the little boys. If only we can make peace & save all the little eighteen-year olds that they are taking every day.

Finally, on 11 November, 1918 Ruth wrote:

The End of the War. It really is true at last; the Armistice was signed at 5 oclock this morning ... Still we cld hardly believe it until we got a paper & all the buzzas began to go, answering the bells, & the sun shone, & people hoisted flags, & there was such a noise & wonder & all quite true at last. So we all shook hands & announced a holiday, for the war actually stopped at eleven, just before we got the news. For an hour or two or three – I hardly know, I was walking about ... there was such a crowd before the Town Hall all the time, & the bells ding-donging away, so that if the Lord Mayor had made a speech no one could have heard him possibly. Then we went to Lawson's and to Tilleys to get sweets for Hope's [her sister's] play centre children. We got two lbs plain for them; & then we ... had coffee at Tilleys – which I don't think I've done since the War – the War that is now over. The orchestra played God Save the King & we all stood up; & followed it by other national airs; & the staff cheered. Then we walked about the streets ... such crowds & crowds of people, & little flags, & big flags on all the shops & buildings & crowds of children waving flags, & crowds of children marching with flags & tin cans & guys but I suppose they [the guys] are Kaisers now. And all the people had flags & red & white & blue ribbons, & there was no traffic except now & then a big car or motor dray loaded with munition girls or wounded soldiers or festooned with flags; & the NER [North Eastern Railway] men were letting the little dirty children ride in swarms in the empty rulleys. All the cars had stopped & the tramway men & girls came marching down the street singing, & as I was at lunch at Carricks, fine decorated [tram] cars, packed with drivers & conductresses went down Grainger Street, cheering & waving. People would cheer for anything & every here & there were soldiers giving away scraps of paper ribbon red white & blue for favours, & people mobbing round in thick crushes to get a bit ... I went into St John's [church] to give thanks & afterwards into the Cathedral ... And this is my last War Journal.

Right: Crowds gather for the Peace Day Parade marching up Grainger Street, 19 July 1919. Ten thousand troops and volunteers took 40 minutes to pass the saluting point. Other events on Peace Day included a concert at St James's Park and huge bonfire on the Town Moor.

Victory parties.

(This page) Top left: Clifford Street, Byker, 1918. Right: Heaton, 1919. Above: Spring 1919, note the fancy dress.

(Next page) Top: Unknown location, 1918. Bottom: more fancy dress at Rochester Street. 1918.

The celebrations lasted for around a year, with every street in Newcastle holding victory teas or peace teas.

In 1923 Newcastle saw the unveiling of two war memorials. *The Response*, at Barras Bridge in the grounds of the Civic Centre, was designed by Sir William Goscombe John RA and depicts soldiers marching off to war. Their wives and children wave goodbye as an angel watches over them. The raised inscription on the front reads '*non sibi sed patriae*', meaning 'not for self, but for country'. The memorial was commissioned by Sir George (a local ship owner) and Lady Renwick. Thankfully, all five of their sons returned from the war. It has been described by former Director General of the Imperial War Museum, Alan Borg, as one of the finest sculptural ensembles on any British monument and was chosen by Royal Mail as one of the images used on stamps commemorating the centenary of the Great War.

In Old Eldon Square, Field Marshal Sir Douglas Haig unveiled a memorial featuring a large bronze statue of Saint George, the patron saint of infantrymen and cavalrymen, slaying the dragon. It was designed by Charles Leonard Hartwell. Appeals raised £16,374 4s 4d to build the memorial but the total cost was £13,260, so the balance was donated to the Royal Victoria Infirmary to provide extra beds for the treatment of ex-servicemen.

Gateshead's war memorial, which stands on the junction of Durham Road and Prince Consort Road, was unveiled in May 1922 by the Lord Bishop of Durham. It records 1,565 names of those who died in the First World War. The tall stone structure, designed by J.W. Spink, features a bronze relief of a classical warrior, sculpted by Captain Richard Reginald Goulden. Below the relief is a teak door that leads to the room of remembrance. The room used to contain a book of remembrance resting on a stone lectern. The book is now housed in Gateshead Library. The memorial cost £5,459 to build and the additional money raised was donated to the children's hospital.

Above: Gateshead's war memorial contains a room of remembrance. Right top: The Response unveiled by the Prince of Wales, 5 July 1923. Right below: Field Marshal Haig unveiled the City's War Memorial in Eldon Square a few weeks later on 26 September 1923.

A note on the sources

The author would like to thank the following people for permission to quote extensively from their published and unpublished work:

Maureen Calcott: Pilgrimage of Grace: The Diaries of Ruth Dodds 1905-1974 *Bewick Press, 1995.*

Ruth Dodds was born in Gateshead in 1890 and lived all her life at her family home in Low Fell. Her father, Edwin, was the owner of a printing business on Newcastle Quayside. Ruth was educated in Gateshead and at boarding school in London. During the war she worked (as many other middle-class women did) as a part-time munitionette at Armstrongs, then moved to her father's print works as more and more male workers were called up for armed service. Ruth's wartime diaries paint a vivid picture of her own and her friends' experiences at home and overseas. Maureen Calcott points out that the war had a profound effect on Ruth. Her pre-war diaries show a girl preoccupied with clothes, dances, tennis parties and her footballing heroes from Newcastle United. During the war she developed an urge to be socially useful and after the end of hostilities she joined both the Labour Party and the Society of Friends. She became a Labour Councillor in 1929 and was editor of the *Gateshead Labour News* (later the *Gateshead Herald*).

Maureen Calcott: 'Arms and the Woman: Women and the War Industries on Tyneside 1914-1918'. Northern History, 2010.

This article examines the dramatic changes that the war made to womens' work outside the home. It contains many first-hand descriptions of women's war experiences, including those of Ruth Dodds.

Brian Dalkin: The Diaries of Isabel Scoon, nee Dalkin, 1887-1982.

Isabel Dalkin was 26 when war broke out. During the conflict she lived with her family in Bristol Terrace, Elswick. Her father was managing director of a cattle auctioneering company in Newcastle. Isabel did not work outside the home but seems to have been responsible for much of the housework, mentioning everything from laundry to baking in her diary. She was no drudge, however, and had many friends and a lively social life. She was particularly fond of the theatre and cinema and enjoyed long drives and cycle rides. Many of her male friends (including her fiancé, later husband, Rankin Scoon) served in the forces. Although Isabel kept a diary for most of her life, she stopped writing in October 1916 and there are no more diaries until 1939.

Isabel died in November 1982 aged 95. Her nephew, Brian Dalkin helped with the clearance of her upstairs flat in Gainsborough Grove, Fenham where the diaries were found, he says: 'We stuffed them into two biscuit tins that were pushed into the bottom of a wardrobe. Thirty years later I decided to take a look. The Diaries ran from 1905 up to 1976, but unfortunately many of them were unreadable due to either fading ink or 'bleeding'. I was left with two 'runs', 1905 to 1916 and 1949 to 1976. I decided to transcribe the diaries from 1905 to 1916 which included the First World War.'

Anthony Flowers: Basil Bunting: A Northern Life *by Richard Caddel and Anthony Flowers, Tyne Bridge Publishing, 1997.*

Basil Bunting was born in Scotswood, Newcastle in 1900. Brought up as a Quaker, in 1918 he was arrested and imprisoned as a conscientious objector. He later became a noted modernist poet and his most famous poem, *Briggflats*, was published in 1966

Thomas Hewitson: A Soldier's Life: The Story of Newcastle and its Barracks, *Tyne Bridge Publishing, 1999.*

This book tells the story of the rise and decline of the military presence in Newcastle upon Tyne. Newcastle Barracks has housed many thousands of troops, often along with their families, from the dashing hussars of Napoleonic times to the Tommies of the two World Wars, and the National Servicemen of recent history. Thomas Hewitson quotes from the unpublished memoirs of Harry Fellows, a volunteer who joined the Northumberland Fusiliers at Newcastle in September 1914.

Thanks are also due to Ken Smith, who generously allowed me access to his invaluable research on Tyneside shipyards during the First World War.

Isabel Dalkin and Rankin Scoon. (Brian Dalkin)